Fruit Box Castles:

Poems From
a Peach Rancher's Daughter

poems by

Jennifer O'Neill Pickering

Finishing Line Press
Georgetown, Kentucky

Fruit Box Castles:

Poems From a Peach Rancher's Daughter

—For dad, mother and grandparents—
Thank you for your sharing the gift of nature.

Copyright © 2020 by Jennifer Pickering
ISBN 978-1-64662-311-2 First Edition
All rights reserved under International and Pan-American Copyright Conventions. No part of this book may be reproduced in any manner whatsoever without written permission from the publisher, except in the case of brief quotations embodied in critical articles and reviews.

ACKNOWLEDGMENTS

"A Lucky Girl," *Paddock Review* 2019, *Cosumnes River Journal*, 2015
"Bountiful," *Poydras Review*, 2020
"The Apron," *Cosumnes River Journal* V.9, 2015
"Children Are Like Rivers," *News and Review*, 2011
"Grandma Bessie," *The Voices Project*, 2015
"Crann: and "Samsara" *The Orchards Poetry Journal*, 2018
"An Accidental Habitat," *Medusa's Kitchen*, 2011
"First Harvest," *Cosumnes River Journal* V.8, 2014
Sable and Quill: the visual art and writing of writers who are also artists, 2013
"Conversations," *Restore and Restory*, 2012
"Global Warming," *Earth in Here*, 2014

Publisher: Leah Maines
Editor: Christen Kincaid
Cover Art: Mike D. Pickering and Jennifer O'Neill Pickering
Author Photo: Mike D. Pickering

Order online: www.finishinglinepress.com
also available on amazon.com

Author inquiries and mail orders:
Finishing Line Press
P. O. Box 1626
Georgetown, Kentucky 40324
U. S. A.

Table of Contents

Bountiful 1
A Lucky Girl 2
Daddy Left Mama 3
Barefoot 4
The Apron 5
A California History Lesson 6
Children Are Like Rivers 7
Grandma Bessie 8
Leopold is Missing 9
Blessing 10
On the Day They Were Born 11
Crann 12
Do What My Brothers Got Too Do 13
An Accidental Habitat 14
Fruit Box Castles 15
Samsara 16
River Spirit Walk 17
A Winey Poem 18
First Harvest 19
Repurposed Brick Patio 20
Global Warming 21
Alchemy of Grief 22
While I kneel In My Yard Planting Foxgloves 23
Off North Butte Road 24
Fly Fishing 25
A Mother's Sadness Writes A Daughter's Poem 26
How to Cultivate Gardens of Words 27
9066 28
The Cannery 29
El Rey Rojo (The Red King) 30
Before We Had Breasts 31
Poppies In February 32
Imperfect Wheel or Your Science is a Lie 33
Paradise Lost 34
Conversations 35

Bountiful

Mom midwifed rows of freestones
Late July we'd sit under umbrellas of the walnut tree
peeling pink ribbons of skin
release pits in a curl of wrists
Peaches filled canning jars clicking and clacking in caldrons of water
pale circles of paraffin floated on bountiful mouths
November we'd tug the light's chain
creep down the grouchy stairs
to the basement's crochet of spider webs
scatter whatever, behind steamer trunks that stored secrets:

kimonos wrapped in tissue paper, waiting an occasion,
the dragon tea pot, a formal table,
helmets pitted by shrapnel, uniforms grown too small
letters in cursive, a wedding gown, a first mistake;
On one wall summer saved in jars: green beans,
pickles, yellow hearts of peaches;
Mom stopped canning and I could never fit into her waders
use the watery screen of an I pad to recipe words—
can memories—picked ripe in season

honest labor.

A Lucky Girl

She is the youngest daughter
the good listener,

the lucky one with straight
teeth, the last born,
not often given to advice.
People tell her their secrets.

Before Dad ran off to Mexico,
with the best friend,
the older sister never had
much to say about life at *Farmlands*;
the high-water bungalow,
twenty-acres of tomatoes,
stewing in summer's kettle.
How she skips right through his warnings
Don't go down to the river.

Never speaks of the whippings,
behind the barn,
except to the little sister,
the good listener.
How it takes forever to unhook his belt,
the one with the horseshoe buckle.
How she braces for the sting
against the planks of bubbled paint.
leather to soft skin
tattooed with welts
as if she just stepped on a wasps nest,

and not out of line.

Daddy Left Mama
(a song)

Daddy Left Mama before I was born
left her with two kids on a two-bit peach farm.
Ran off with another had raven black hair
left Mama pregnant two babes she would bear.
Daddy was a dreamer this I was told
looking for greener pastures
that had already been sold
went down to Mexico with all mamas' dough
grew cotton in Sonora but never struck gold.

Chorus
*Now a love can turn fickle this surely is true
and someone is always gonna' lose
when the red heart of passion mixes with blue
and a heart becomes purple—just like a bruise.*

Well I didn't see my Daddy till I was just three
and that isn't how it is meant to be
when he held me in arms I wailed and cried
Cause even a wee one knows when a Daddy's lies.

Repeat Chorus
I forgave my daddy after callin' him every word
in the dictionary that was dirtier than dirt.
I'll be dammed if I didn't become like him—possibly worse
a dreamer paintin' pictures writin'—verse.

Barefoot

The day we buried mother
tule fog settled on the morning of a weak sun
lines between what was known
and imagined blurred
wind held its tongue
crested sparrows forgot their verse
the sky wept without rain
I deliver the bundle of clothes to the mortuary
a best dress, the good leather purse, a lace slip
forgot her shoes

always the first thing she'd kick off after work
how she arrived into this world,
how she'd leave in comfort.

The Apron

Her mother's gift
years fray the lace
pretty faded floral print,
clouds of bleach stains;
strings tied with a flourish
into pink bows around the waist
she's battled for years.

shielding
favorite jeans, t shirts,
going-out-kicking-up-her-heals-skirts,
holiday vests,
what it could not:
the wound over her heart,
a first husband the cemetery keeps,
sons to the Iraq War,
a daughter married too soon,
one given to drink.

The apron holds what the day offers:
lost toys, zinnias' red heads, tears,
stray kittens, a finch's repose
cell phones, winter greens,
toddlers' sticky fingers,
what's left behind—

What's discovered.

A California History Lesson

I'm asked to be content with my urban space; its picket fence surrounding fruitless trees silhouettes aligned with distant granite peaks of mirrored glass the migratory birds' mistake for sky. The new habitat of hawks hunting pigeon and crow nested in iron beams or in the tallest English Sycamore marooned in contrived meadows of Bermuda grass. My history bound in comfortable complacency frozen into the stone eyes, the sour smiles captured in tin photographs ancestors sailing from Dublin and Amsterdam to Norfolk and Philadelphia with hearts carrying a longing to feel solidity even more than hope or bread to tame the growls of their children's empty bellies and the loss of leaving everything that was so much of nothing but, familiar; forbearers shuffling westward towards the horizon in a momentum that could not be slowed. from Missouri to Oregon swallowing dust, pride, the stink of oxen mired in the Platt River mud bound in stays and soles of worn out boots stuffed with prairie grass, burying babies, sorrow and broken Majolica in potato fields following the up and down of mountains to home in the great valley at the foot of the coast range, violet as the iris gardens left behind, to the country of the Wintu and Maidu whose stands of grass summer polish like the gold tips of gentlemen's walking sticks beaten down by a government handing out land like hard candy, as if it were theirs to give-the Welsh, Scotch, Irish, and Germans—farmers, ranchers sailing in prairie schooners uprooted from their own land by greed, law, civil wars starvation that set blood against blood women's lye soap would not wash clean—history being a stubborn stain you see. Good land for those who would plow it and set their grazing sheep and cattle on its sweet grass to pay its taxes. Even now the Red-tailed hawks feathered fingers outline stands of Red Bud stirred awake in a February of too much rain—flinging the white lace of almond blossoms on cerulean canvases—sugaring an earth dark with secrets.

Children Are Like Rivers

when you try to straighten them out
they might go along with you for awhile
then, they'll jump their banks
to snatch back their wild.
All you really need to do is:
widen their boundaries
let and them meander.

Grandma Bessie

i.

Grandma left school after eighth grade
when more hands were needed for the dairy
took her place next to her mother
squatting on stools coaxing milk
from sour faced cows
loved to write stories

gave it up after marriage
to a man with ambition
camping in an army tent
at her brother's orange grove
saving money for *their* dairy.

They grew to hate the cows
sold everything after he
bluffed his way through
his third-grade education
into a line foreman at Harter's cannery

ii.

You'd never know
she'd just chopped off hen's head
was on her hands and knees
picking strawberries big as apples
knew her way around the Smith and Wesson
a better shot than her husband

was a lady who hadn't
married someone with no Iota about business
wore her best suit to town,
pinned with a rhinestone brooch
cocked the feathered hat just so,
clutched the pocketbook
with smooth gloved hands   covered the calluses.

Leopold Is Missing

Leopold is missing a proud rooster who greets the
granddaughter the same as when he was a chick clucks
and struts and pecks at the handout in her pockets.

He explored the orchard with her showing off
alighting in fruit trees—upstaging the sparrows
even the grey Tom cat knows his place.

Grandmother has warned her not to befriend
the domesticated animals.
But Aunt Lila has told her differently.
Her rabbits love her.
Holding them next to her heart
smoothing their silky coats,
they pass over unafraid humming contentedly.

She has a quick wrist and keeps her blades sharpened
Like Ann Boleyn's French executor
so quick he was with the blade his victims died smiling.

Grandma's mums dazzle a chipped Briggle vase with a story of its own
gracing the table at Sunday dinner.
She's known for her fried chicken guests are coming,
that Grandpa needs to impress.

The granddaughter hides the leg beneath mashed potatoes
swallows a poisonous tongue—asks politely to be excused
before showers of tears betray true feelings
slips something into her pocket;

Outside under the hunter moon, tears bright as diamonds, she
fetches a shovel buries a small part of Leopold in the orchard
at the roots of his favorite tree.

Blessing

Blessed with a blossoming heart
with summer flowers seeded in spring
in this garden of wild, native, exotic, and tame;
this pitcher of morning light
poured across the wooden planks
Cannas' umbrella of leaves;
the walnut's basket of nuts
squirrels' steady harvest
mandalas of black-eyed Susan fringed in gold
sycamores and breeze linked in song.

Blessed with sparrows' passion to sing,
hummingbirds' endurance, inquisitive jays,
afternoon baptisms quiver of wings
release of sorrow
space that cultivates joy;
feelings turned over
like the trowel amends;
the yin yang
sadness and joy
different and the same.

On the Day They Are Born

the lilac blouse of dawn buttons up the moon.
Grandpa's boots plod rice stubble
course as his, three days without a shave.
Shotgun shells clatter over the frozen fields
flush pheasants into the sulphur air.

Grandma smoothes starched sheets
on a daughter's cast iron bed
alone, since he'd left for Mexico.
Grandma saw he was trouble from the start.
The daughter smitten blind to the ambush
Grandma won't let her forget.

North wind came up and blew the gate open
and the goat got into the yard
trimming the beards of the purple irises.
The daffodils would be next,
dawning foolish straw hats
like it was a picnic in summer.

They'd wanted a boy.
She arrived first kicking and screaming,
a brother second.
Twins that surprised everyone,
not expected to live,
incubated back to health, came home in a week.
Their other brother, no longer the baby pouted
older sister, a reluctant third mother.

A Red Hawk dipped its wings
like polite folks did their hats
nose dived scooping up a field mouse.
Lightning split the heavens open,
blew away the calm of the afternoon.
Rain drummed the new tin roof
announced their arrival.

Crann

More trees than Paris
shade of infinite joy
marriage of earth and sky
rungs to paradise.

The house was chosen for
the old sycamore the city gave away
branches grown yard to yard
touching tentatively as new lovers.
The house is simple in design
made of bones of trees—a sacred place.

Her ancestors cradled apple saplings coming west
purchased at nurseries in Missouri and Ohio
precious as the heirlooms left behind.
These they'd plant with raised barns
for pressed cider potent as whiskey.

As a girl she lived on an island of yard
surrounded by oceans of trees whose
April blossoms spun dreams.
The apricot, a favorite to climb
flatten limb to limb
match its shape.

When the developer uprooted
the almond orchard across the road
one linked with a swing,
she wept for hideouts dug
in leafy shade roofs of scrap wood
wattle of mud and Johnson grass

refuge gone in a day.

Do what My Brothers Got to Do

When I was ten I wanted to
do what my brothers got to do:
kill things living or dead,
bucks, squirrels, piles of rocks,
gophers, beer bottles,
hook trout, catfish and their finger,
spit luggies, burn rubber on the John Deere,
be waited on by the women,
drink grandpa's whiskey, grimace,
start fights in the parking lot of
the Pump House Bar,
try to kick the cat, smoke Marlboros,
shout four letter words,
leave dirty underwear on the floor,
get grease under my nails, in my teeth and hair
replacing a carburetor,
drive without a license—
whistle with two fingers real loud.

An Accidental Habitat

Two mallards, a husband and wife,
have taken up residence in the park
with the crows and hawks poised
in watchful grace.
What are the draws?
Firearms prohibited signs—
A concrete pond sloshing with rainfall.

We watch their waddle
toward water
return to the green
after the sprinklers shut off
and armies of angle worms
surface for air.

The couple rejoices
in this impromptu marsh
flap napkins of wings,
feast.

Fruit Box Castles

Too young to understand ranching
I was the observer with a head full of questions
getting in the way as Grandma pulled on her waders,
sloshed down the muddy rows.

shoveled open the checks gridding the orchard in dirt geometry
Summers we slept on cots unfolded in screened porches;
The hum of the water pump switching on and off lulled us to sleep
told never play on the 2x4's covering the well—or meet the calico's fate
fished up in the net, a wet mop of meows.

Late summer meant fruit box castles, children's' architectural wonders
towers prodding the gates of heaven;
When the limbs dropped toward the earth heavy with fruit
Grandma braced them with wooden props of v's.
culled the smallest for canning and peach pies.

The crew came to harvest in a cloud of cinnamon dust
sunburned faces peeked out from checkered bandanas
beneath straw hats, magicians' hands filled canvas sacks and
once an infant in a smaller sack nursed as a mother
relieved the lower branches of their fruit.

Grandma counted boxes; Grandpa drove, the tractor towed the flatbed
to the men with biceps like the trunks of oaks, stacking pallets.
Afterwards the orchard looked roughed up
as if there had been theft or violation.

Samsara
    Paying respect to my Dad's ashes at Scott's Flat Lake, Nevada City, C.A.

A cold warmth beneath sky
grey as a cats' fur
licks the air with saltshakers of snow.
A Sierra February colors my cheeks
like wild strawberries in summer.
I look for you in the clear depths of the lake
at the quartz and obsidian sisters
tumbled smooth by the current's cradle
imagine a small bone held in place:
that I might make a wish upon
think I hear the aria of your laughter
north wind carries up the ridge
into the chantey of pines.
I want to cry, but my eyes are stones
skipping across the tin skin of lake.
I hear you call out my name in a flat horned note
the splash of a strong swimmer (as you'd been).
Is this mud hen, this duck your samsara—eager for my bread crumbs?
How easily she glides, shelters in the alder's crochet of twigs
warm in her feathered bed.

The Hindus process of reincarnation is called samsara, a continuous cycle in which the soul is reborn over and over again according to the law of action and reaction. At death many Hindus believe the soul is carried by a subtle body into a new physical body which can be a human or non-human form (an animal or divine being).

River Spirit Walk

The red-tailed hawk maps the blue meander
wings the updraft between canyons of mirrored towers
swoops above the green riparian ribbon
refuge of coyote and bobcat inking footnotes in clay
with native scribes preceding our own;
We walk through cottonwood's snow of seeds, grass knee deep
duvet to fawn and doe, groves of oak fruiting acorns and galls
to the parting of the alders at a point bar where
minnows spark the eddied pools turtles sun
on forgotten wharfs otters
somersault in shadowed pools
Chinook journey to the sea opalescent river jewels.

A Winey Poem

They were a perfect blend—a first crush
a doux du tart, an one handy with a corkscrew
made each other blush
grew drunk on Sangria, each other and plonk
until they afforded the expensive reserve
(if only they could have bottled what they had.)

But alas, they didn't age well.
When did the noble rot begin?
When did one become so flabby
and the other a brut?
How had they both become bungs and cold ducks?

One of them thought,
I care not about bright—feel like something pink or bubbly—
a Blanc de Noirs, an overture
that plays a champagne flute—
that will pop my cork, make a hole
in this mid-life crisis and (the ceiling).

That "something" slipped off the shelf at Trader Joes.
The jilted lover thought, that will soon go flat,
sought complexity, stillness experimented with Sack and Sherry
explored varietals, embraced the abboccato;

Settled on fruity with hint of spice, naughty with a nice finish
decided most were just wet dickies anyway
and took a lesson from the wine to breathe!

First Harvest
(ekphrasis poem after viewing Pears, by Renaldo Cuneo)

Before the skies pepper with fowl
the first hard freeze she climbs the knoll
booted feet the muddy road
complaint of knees
basket slung on flannelled arm
the farmwoman's charm bracelet

Fog cobwebs the orchard
noon sun brooms away
surveys a family's labor
a daughter's inheritance

She chooses Mirabelles, Bartlett, Anjous, Bosc
for their fragrance: honey and spice
imperfect skins conceal pale sweet flesh
chooses for color: lutescent coppery, sumac red,
those blushed by summer's constant gaze
for their song of curves

for how they fill an empty hand.

The Repurposed Brick Patio

i.

Twenty years, the tree had made them sneeze
four weeks in the spring and in the fall before a good rain
grenades of fluff strung on limbs
the sun ignited carried in explosions of wind.

They disliked the bark's messy sloughing skin
the leathery leaves large as open hands
overflowing the green waste bins
camouflaging sidewalks ankle deep in the yard
labor intensive and too abundant.

Squirrels favored the sycamore's canopy for their nests of fall leaves
made water proof with plastic bags gathered on a recycle day
in the middle branches jays preened,
two-tone coats of blue, argued incessantly
until crows smudged charcoal wings on dusk skies
home to roost in a cottonwood at the river.

Mid-winter as the tree slept in capes of tule fog
not old enough to be a heritage tree they cut it down
built their patio of repurposed brick.
Besides, there was still the Blue oak
that thrives despite neglect.
Why had they waited so long?

ii.

"Why did you cut down my longtime companion?
Seven years we survived the drought.
Forty years of healing shade
summers here that fry eggs.
What of gratitude?"

The oak bides her time, plots revenge
spreads her roots becomes a heritage tree.
Cracks the pretty patio like a six on the Richter scale,
until there is no joy reclined on chaise lounges
smearing brie on crackers, sipping Pinot Grigio,
Would the house be next?

Global Warming

This morning on the plaza in front of the church
choirs of starlings sound the alarm
from canopies of sycamores risen in lakes of brick and stone.
I negotiate the worn trail in clickety-clackety heels
to the watering hole where there is frenzy for French roast.
The air is thick as cream and sweet with jasmine
almost camouflages whiffs of urine in the door wells.

A sky rumbles angry, as she bears.
Lightening will be next.
I know this from summers in Wichita
followed by a steady sobbing of clouds.
Strange weather for California in August.

But then, so were whales in the river last spring
bringing out moms with strollers
and beer bellied men camped in lawn chairs
bevies of barefoot children
risking muddy banks wielding sodas and hot dogs.
Present to feed a hunger for magic
missing in the sermons on social media.

We cheer the finned family on,
their journey of healing
Madonna and child
speaking a language of hope.
Some of us pray
others track their progress
on *Google Earth*
aghast that they swim toward Mt. Shasta.

We applaud the wounded explorers change in direction
following the river's pulse through a delta's venation out to sea.

The Alchemy of Grief

In theory we begin our journeys at birth.
Travel backwards moving forward.
Observation is vital to the outcome of an experiment.
To turn grief, a solid, into tears
or feelings calcified to a simple solution

or to do right by a mother
takes time measured with divination.
Commit your findings to page.
Weigh the variables against the constant values.

Test their viability formulate tinctures, potions for sleep.
Collect tears in crystal beakers. Use what is required.
Release them to nights devoid of stars,
someone who needs to cry.

Below you will find several conclusions I am certain are true:
Data based on emotions is impossible to validate.
Sadness cannot be measured by liters.
Often what we know is understood as fact
and can never be proven scientifically.

While I Kneel in My Yard Planting Foxgloves

giving thanks to spring, the Mother's grit under my nails;
My neighbor says my yard is a meadow landscape.

He, with his minimalist crushed granite creation dotted with potted
drought tolerant plants make me feel a little ashamed of my weeping shrubs—

the mallow skirting the ground blooms of violet centered stars;
His tub of bluebells, a fall gift, ring when the wind comes up

surprise the bridle wreath whose petals salt mulched earth;
Dutch iris sprung up over night with the of lengthening sun's rays
warrant broad-brimmed straw hats.

I vow to plant Red Buds, milkweed and Pipevines, host plants for swallowtails
and monarchs, natives conserving our scarce water;

Honeysuckle and Lilac pond my eyes with tears
I cultivate too much sweetness that spurs memories of funeral homes—
loved ones laid out as is my people's custom.

I never much liked these displays—my niece looking like a large puffy doll,
drowning does this to the body the coroner said, sixteen, with strawberry lips
and cheeks to match—only her hair looked alive as a wildfire.

I wonder how Stephon Clarke looks across town.
How did they stitch closed the bullet holes? Can such loss ever be filled?

How did they make him look handsome as the church usher,
the proud father, a mother's son, a brother?

Not the gunned-down bullet-ridden grandson hunted into
the sanctuary of his Grandma's spring yard.

Do his children kiss his cheek to find only the cold of winter?

Off North Butte Road

i.
Fog
hems the earth
threads needles of light
sews running stitches
wind, the final unraveling.

ii.
rice stubbles the fields
flooded with winter pools
mirrors a turquoise
umbered and swirled in gold
everywhere song of swan, and mallards

iii.
notes sung from manuscripts of sky
herald spring
those who commit for life
wing to heaven
in a complex geometry
without gps or compass
return home.

Fly Fishing

Grandfather was a patient teacher.
There was no more gifted orator
on the fly, trade secrets
netted in her braids,
tucked beneath a straw hat
with the marabou jig.

Summers he'd demonstrate the way
to bait a hook, when to troll,
with the right bait:
nymphs, dillys, Velveeta.
Follow the moon's phases,
leading to the deepest pools,
catch and release what needed
to lengthen another season.

She gave up the pole
never getting her limit,
reel in the elusive lunger,
fishing in ponds of words,
streams of consciousness,
following in his footsteps,

another pursuit that cannot be hurried.

Mother's Silence Writes a Daughter's Poem

They lean against the flatbed truck
her hair escapes a bandanna
both in overalls.
his straw hat half cocked
arms chained,
smiles bright as charms.

Winter mother sews hope
into gingham curtains
crochets thimble sized shoes
pieces together squares
into pastel blankets
craves pickles and honey
keeps busy.

Named for their father she is still born
first born, sister the siblings won't know
tumble of crimson curls
on a satin pillow pink as taffy.

Here clergy spoke lovely words
for the family, she
in a box so small
the mourners call her porcelain doll.
The mother's silence writes the daughter's poem.

Trembling Stars grow quilts to warm you
where olive orchards once grew
and families of crows dressed in mourning
harvest the fruit from those trees that remain.

Day's Eyes watch over you now
sparrows sing eves songs
from the choir stalls of cedar boughs.
Guardian angels spread marbled wings
frozen in eternal flight.

How to Cultivate Gardens of Words

Begin with fertile ground,
an assortment of possible themes.
Plant your seedlings with care.
Marvel at how fast they grow.
Sharpen your tools.
Prepare to develop calluses.
Sow handfuls of words
to propagate chapters.

Pray to the garden
and at the touch screen to
Seshat, Gaia, and Demeter.
Dig in.
Calculate depth accurately.
Rake over the plots several times.
Surround yourself with beauty,
diversity, the wild, native and exotic.

Leave generous spaces for trailers.
Lattice the climbing rhyme.
Study the moon's phases
planting with intention in season.
Plan for the unpredictable:
bolting, dampening off,
too much rain, the dry spells.

Weed selectively.
Cull over your thoughts.
Make a ritual of thinning.
Work when you do not want to
near songbirds,
the laughter of children.
Wear a hat .seated in silence.

Consult the Farmer's Almanac
the dictionary.
Use the thesaurus
to replace wilted words
that can't stand up to the heat.
The flowering will arrive.
Ready your baskets
for bumper crops.

9066

Someone mows a lawn.
Its cologne sweetens the afternoon.
She is again six planted in a slow ordinary day
before she understood the word nuclear
before the Bay of Pigs
The Kennedy's were shot followed by Dr. King.
they draft her first love to Nam
and vets comes back broken
from undeclared wars.
After Pearl Harbor and headlines of fear
a Good Deal President signs into law
and they round up neighbors down the road
confiscate their almond orchards;
playmates prodded onto trains
shipped like cattle to Manzanar
corralled behind bales of barbed wire.
Grownups' whispers of: "spies, yellow tide, Nisei, "
climb the stairs.

The Cannery

My mother like hers worked in the cannery, in the valley where mountains loomed distant and snowcapped even in the hot breath of summer. My mother, each dawn, shuffled off in white uniformity, a nurse of fruit, ten hour days, swing shifts, glad for a break the quick smoke; the belt an infinite dark line repeating it's dumb path; The hands that burn with the sweet juice of peaches were meant to write, feet, aching and stationary to run; legs spoiled, meant to dance; Women have smaller hands they'd say, are more adept at sorting the bad from the good and pay was good for valley towns with names that rolled off your tongue like the notes in a mariachi band; Delano, Modesto, Sacramento—where jobs were scarce as shade.

El Rey Rojo (The Red King)

If I hadn't called you el Rey Rojo
hadn't filled the birdfeeder con las semillas de girasol
watched your flaming breast in joyful splash of wings
while I plucked the golden tassels
off spring bulbs, readied for summer.
If I'd left birdbaths dry hadn't made this
pequeno habitat nestled in an urban sprawl
if we'd let the neighbors cut down the gnarled walnut tree
ruck its emerald canopy, if it hadn't been a drought
if I could live with reservoirs of guilt
turn away thirsty birds in el cielo hot as Hades
dropping like stones from sooty skies
spawned on flumes of forest fires
if I'd gathered up the wild plums—simmered them for winter jam
and if you'd not been so guapo amigo emplumado
in your vest the color de pasion
made my head turn—if our eyes had not met
if I'd turned mine away— made you stay afraid
not of me, for what I offer;
longing to save, to study, to tame
as is our foolish human way.
If I hadn't heard the hawk's cry because her children starve
though your sacrifice won't ease their hunger pains
you are not their savior slipped from a mother's grasp
to another mother's arms resting with the flowering
maple, their crimson tolling bells
as is fitting for El Rey Rojo!

Translation: Sunflower seeds, small, sky, feathered handsome friend, the color of passion

Before We Had Breasts

grandmother tried to reel
us in with the hook of her tongue,
afraid we'd drown
free-styling to deep water
slicing wave's of milky meringue
flaked with driftwood
swam the backstroke.
floated chests pressed
to blue domes of sky
propellers of feet
in lemon light
dived beneath logs of sugar pine
tied with ribbons of steel
surprised catfish, big as dogs.

Poppies in February

Are you sunrise's ubade
Olwen's daughter's
flames singeing dark holes in flannel clouds
You do not burn my jeaned legs or ungloved hands
shaking loose you opiate perfume

These gray taped up days
 seal out the light
petals fold up
steady rains unfurl
your golden parasols
the first to
brighten farmers' stubbly fields
the mediums of the highways north
my winter mood.

I learned as a child of your true value
not this bouquet of illegal gold spent
in a Roseville vase
set in the ring of this polished table top
but in the long wait after the rains leave
ten thousand ebony seeds
delivered to the mother's dark vaults
with combinations she keeps.

Imperfect Wheel or Your Science Is a Lie

Stopped at the red light,
I study the sturdy scaffold of your trunk and limbs
angled toward the sun, tree top an imperfect wheel
wakes on the wind's currents, mystery
of green embryos safe in wooden wombs,
the feathered minstrels journey still,
no spring soloist lights your branch to cheer the grey afternoons.

I wonder if you regret your lot: planted between two freeways
doomed to semis' rumbles, the belch of commuters,
the zigzag whirr of cyclists getting somewhere quick.
Your only companions the redwood welcoming Tule fog
The native lilac April shakes awake.

Would you rather reflect in a farmer's pond, gaze across alfalfa fields,
keep a backyard tree house, raucous with children's laughter?
Have you forgiven the gardener who staked you upright
planted you in this artificial burn?
Do you welcome eve's cacophony of crows ripe as figs
urban hawks eye, perched on solar powered poles
these men, unfurling sleeping bags calling your roots home.

Is your answer the firm handshake of sky,
the Mother's tithe each fall,
July's shade, your persistent pursuit of pure air,
though we are told your science is a lie?

Paradise Lost

Sky rains ash
grays snow white hair
salts and peppers the Lab, a stray born
with the North star on his chest.

She rescued him and now he leads them down charred streets
past blackened bodies of cars, afraid to peer inside
past neighbors' homes dust to dust,
past the forests' funeral pyres;

A President issues blame
his words no salve to ease the victims' loss
coughing and staggering through befouled air
lungs on fire mouths pinned to bandanas;

Nettie blames the 100 mile winds, the stingy autumn rains,
bad luck, maybe climate change, someone's greed;
She prays and hopes her prayers are answered
because she's lapsed.

Midnight limps forward
stops and growls at the smoke screen
flaked, metal and plastic, flesh and bone, water and wood
what lifetimes' grow burn in an hour.

Gabriel in a fireman's helmet, his light a halo
floats towards them,

come to carry them to home.

Conversations

I asked the sky if it defined
the boundary of the barn.
Sky replied," Trust what is seen,
answer all else with faith."

The barn said, "I sit on the earth,
a shelter made from the limbs of a sister oak,
older than I and who once held up the sky."
The spirit of the sister oak said to the barn,
"The sky was never a burden
even resting on my shoulders."

Her son called to the passing squirrel,
"I welcome you across my threshold
as friends do pilgrims, mothers their children."
The squirrel thanked Father Lightning
for opening a door.

A hawk flying by called down,
"If you agree there are no differences
between endings and beginnings,
no boundary will define you."
Then the wind came up, whispering,
"In each breath reside all answers."

Jennifer O'Neill Pickering has deep roots in Northern California and lived on a peach ranch. Some of her ancestors came in covered wagons to California from Missouri in the 1860's.

She is an award winning literary and visual artist. The City of Sacramento selected two of her creative works for two Art in Public Places projects: *I Am the Creek*, a poem is part of the site-specific sculpture, *Open Circle* (Les Birleson). The sculpture is meant to be a place of healing after the synagogue adjacent to it was fire bombed. Her poem, "Affirmation" and visual art from the Goddess Series is included in the *Signal Box Project*. She has been published across the country in, *Restore and Restory: A Peoples History of the Cache Creek Nature Preserve, Yellow Silk, Mt. Akum Review, Heresies, Cosumnes River Journal* and elsewhere.

Her poem, "The Lucky Girl" was nominated for a Pushcart Prize for Poetry. "Paper Prisoner" was awarded the best California state worker poem in a contest sponsored by the *Suttertown News*. She was a finalist in the New Women's Voices Chapbook Competition, Finishing Line Press.

Find her prose in *The Arlington Literary Journal, The Dog with the Old Soul, Raven's Perch, Restore and Restory: A Peoples History of the Cache Creek Nature Preserve,* and elsewhere. She is a board member of the Sacramento Poetry Center, the Editor of the *Sable and Quill: The visual art and writing of writers who are also artist v.1* and curates the Poets' Gallery.

Jennifer has taught art and writing at colleges, homeless shelters and in public schools, performed her poetry on stage at the Sophia, California State University Sacramento. the Old Eagle Theater, art galleries, and elsewhere. She was awarded several grants and fellowships for teaching, writing and visual art from the Sacramento Metropolitan Art Commission and was the recipient of the Robert Else Increase Robinson Fellowship at California State University Sacramento. She holds an MA in Studio Art from California State University Sacramento, was an undergraduate at the University of New York at Buffalo and is a graduate of the Artist's Residency Institute for Teaching Artists for both literary and visual art.

When not writing and creating art she enjoys riding her Townie, singing, writing songs, hosting events, travel with her family and digging in the community garden. To learn more about Jennifer go to: shepaintsandwrites.com or her blog: Jennifer's Art and Words.

www.ingramcontent.com/pod-product-compliance
Lightning Source LLC
LaVergne TN
LVHW041554070426
835507LV00011B/1081